Drink in the blue sky
Cumulus clouds are floating
Shining sun on them

Other Titles from

**Deborah K. Tash
White Wolf Woman**

Inspired By The Tides

Soft Power/Reclaiming The Sacred Cunt Project

Journal Sketches And Hidden Voices

Harvesting The Moon

Illuminated Poems

Ravens At My Window, Ravens On My Roof, Roses On My Table

108 Dreams Of A Night Poet

Sextets

And Coming Soon:

*The Gods In The Mirror/
An Erotic Adventure Tale Of Spiritual Transformation*

VOICE OF THE POET IN TROUBLED TIMES

DEBORAH K. TASH
WHITE WOLF WOMAN

Published by:

Fumbled Book Press
Oakland, CA

Copyright © 2020 by Deborah K. Tash
In Her Image Studio

All rights reserved. Without limiting rights under copyright reserved above, no part of this book may be reproduced, stored or introduced into a retrieval system, or transmitted, in any form or by any means (electronic, mechanical, photocopying, recording or otherwise), without the prior written permission of both the copyright owner and the publisher.

ISBN: 978-0-9987640-2-3
First Edition: 30JUN2020

Joan and David Lincer, Publishers

Fumbled Book Press brings titles that we know and love back from "Out of Print". Each title is reset with care in Adobe InDesign.

Catalog: www.FumbledBookPress.com

To Howell who encouraged me

Introduction

In the midst of the political turmoil in mid-2019 I began compiling a selection of my poems from my daily writing practice and posting them with images from my photography to create The Voice Of The Poet in Troubled Times. My intention was to share with the readers of my In Her Image Studio newsletter a calm path through the fear and uncertainty we were all navigating with reminders of beauty and the blessings of Spirit in our lives. The photographs are individual reminders and though some of them are paired with Haiku, are meant to stand on their own; not necessarily referring to the poems but adding to the meditative quality.

With the advent of the Covid-19 pandemic and subsequent "shelter in place" mandate here in my San Francisco home resulting in an increase of fear, hysteria and panic it seemed even more essential to share these poems and photos with a wider audience.

For me, being alone for weeks, it has become both a challenge and a treat to adjust to new ways of daily living. I have been learning how to mine the situation for a positive outlook which has led me to go even more deeply into my interior landscape than usual; leading to poems to invoke peace and a more attentive understanding of the blessings of everyday moments.

My hope is that this book of poems and photographs will also bring you comfort, hope and a moment of respite and solace in these troubled times.

Deborah K. Tash
April 2020

Recipe For Dealing With Troubled Times

Gather your ingredients:

In troubled times begin with...
    Counting out all the household things
        you may have overlooked

    Clean water piped into your kitchen
        for a glass filled to the top
    A refrigerator and stove
        for meals that nourish and delight
    A blender
        to make a smoothie or creamed avocado
    A shower when you want to be clean
    Indoor plumbing

    Sheets and warm blankets
    On a bed to sleep in the dark
    Heat when the night is chilled

    All the technology you use each day
    A television
        movies that open your heart
    A radio
        truth telling
    A computer
        to write your story
    A phone or two
        answering your friends' calls

Blend in the sauce of community
      Friendship and those you love
      Remembering the moments of joy
      That got you through other hard times

      When you hear of death
      Think fondly of the dead
      Even if you did not know them
      Give your complete attention to someone else
      Listen to their story
      Remember to hug
      To touch with love

      If you have pets
           stroke them
      If you have children
           tell them you love them

      Tell your friends that you love them
           as often as you can

Measuring out gratitude add liberally to the mix
      You can never have too much thankfulness

Add in the sound of birdsong in the morning
      Flowers and the sweet scents of dawn
      Thankful for another day

Wash your hands and bless them
      Touch with awareness
      Feel your feet on the ground
      Your eyes
      Your ears
      Your nose

Remember to breathe
To speak your truth
Water your plants
Bless your food
Meditate or sit quietly
Walk in nature
Or just stand beneath a tree
Run your hands along its bark
And be grateful for oxygen

And when the trouble feels overwhelming
Add in the spices of the Divine
The sweetness of the Goddess

Look in a mirror into your own eyes
Giving yourself a welcoming smile
      dance at the edge of the ocean with moonlight in your hair
      listen to music
      loud rock and roll
      love songs and ballads
      classical piano
      and all the sounds that soothe your soul
Remember to write love songs and poetry
To sing your own song

Mix it all together and breathe into the moment

19JUL18

Trust

You don't have to judge yourself
Making comparisons to everyone else
Not only are you beautiful as you are
But your life is a gift worth giving

You are kind enough and strong
Loving and generous enough
To recognize jealousy and insecurity
Forgiving them in yourself and others

Lay bare your vulnerable moments
Trusting the power of your connection
Knowing yourself loveable
Even when you are betrayed

Even when you are abandoned
The wound both ancient and present
Still you are enough
Your love wide and potent for forgiveness

28SEP19

You opened the door
To let in the Muse's voice
Now she writes through yours

Welcome Yourself

Welcome yourself into your own heart
Look in the mirror with love
Recognizing your wholeness
Seeing the beauty of your eyes
And forgive yourself for your missteps

Welcome yourself into your future
Casting forward with vision
To shape a life that nurtures you
Fulfilling your dreams with happiness
Finding pleasure in your truth

Welcome yourself into fullness
Blessing your body, mind and spirit
With the sweetness of your being
Letting the river of life carry you
To the land where you belong to yourself

22JAN18

The Unmasking

I am mortified so many times
It seems no matter how much I pray
How often I do or don't meditate and heal
I can't tame the voice of "you're not good enough"

It seems I am relegated
Heaped in the trash
Of my own insistent insecurity
Filled with shame

I want to celebrate others
To revel in their accomplishments
Sing their praises with joy
Not compare myself as less than

And I am mortified by my failure
That mean hissing voice
Turning my heart to stone with jealousy
Even as I struggle to be generous

I want to tell the truth of our shared longings
That we all must tame cruel inner voices
Learn to celebrate ourselves
While countering the meanness of life

09JUL19

The Box

She opened the box reluctantly
Knowing its contents would intensify
Once the cool atmosphere was breached
All the carefully tended protections
Going up in shaking and tears
Leaving that too sensitive skin
Open to the touch of a painful reality

It didn't matter that she'd tended
Hiding it securely in the dark
Faithfully muffling banished grief
To protect what courage she could
Moving forward in a life surviving
Even after tearing down the wall
Clearing out the basement terrors

There was still the box of guilt
Laced around with unreasoning fear
Waiting to be matched by the world
In all its array of cruelty and despair
And how could she encompass it all
Find a path beyond destruction
Once the lid fell back and revealed

But she opened the box anyway
Determined to find passage
To continue through the dark
Feeling the light zephyr
Gently moving toward her
Steadily from the end of the tunnel

19SEP19

Elixir Of The Wind

Deep into the dark
They raged and blew
Winds waking before dawn
To moan and wail

As you drink the elixir
Your chosen path pungent
As the thick herbs brew
Your legs promising

Your legs promising
To walk you into the depths
Of your still hidden power
Harbingers of the wind

With the end so near
Death breathing at your back
And still the winds claim you
Your bones clattering with cold

The messages of pain
Still etched deep into your soul
Waiting to be decrypted
In the gifts of prophecy

Not found in the sweet soft day
Eating and conversation
But in the tasking of alchemy
While the winds howl and threaten

27OCT19

Walking Toward The Sun

Is it only there in the west
Where the sun opens the horizon
Clouds parting in celebration
Of sunset's colorful display
Another day's end before nightfall
Lived and acknowledged

Is it only there in the west
Where the shadow of age
Creeps slowly across the face of it
Exhorting moonlight in its path
Haggard and ailing in time
Demanding more attention to living

Is it only there in the west
Where the sun goes down
Even as we walk steadily toward it
Recognizing the fraying edges
The smudged edges of pleasure
Repeated like a mantra to pain

Is it only there in the west
Walking toward the sun
Can we gather up our losses
Seed them back into the psyche
To be grown like dahlias
For a rich harvest of what is left

20NOV19

In Another Cycle Of The Moon

This is a poem dedicated to pain
All of which we know too well
There is something about it
The accumulation of heartache
Those lineaments of loss
Rigors of survival after betrayal
And the physical ache of chronic hurt
Exacerbated by winter's chill to the bone

There is something about it
Not meant as punishment
Not even a question of what is deserved
But some deep connection to mystery
To the source of spirit embodied
Of endurance and determination to live
Allowing the course of ease
Finding the path to acceptance

The daily task of movement
When pain misunderstood
Would join us to despair
Is a moment carved out of courage
Every cell and sinew alive to its purpose
Willing to plumb the depths
To write a poem also dedicated
Written for the ineffable joy of being

04JAN20

Hibernation

How do you feel in these days
When the light is brewing
One part frigid night
One part desire for sleep

Do you want to hibernate
Sleep pulling down your eyelids
With drowsy winter daydreams
Even when you drift in daylight

Are you ready to sing the darkness
That song of slow turning
Requiring patience for completion
When the days will lengthen

How do you embrace the discontent
That rises in your aching limbs
Calling out your failed hope
When you long for joy

And will you plunge into the wilderness
That ever mysterious region
Standing sentinel at your gates
Til you explore its darkness as your guide

Will you sit silently and allow it
Witness to that mysterious penetration
Aging your skin but bringing prophecy
"Know thyself" written above the entrance

How do you feel in these days
Are you half awake
Half dreaming of unknown worlds
While your body longs for hibernation

03JAN20

The Way We Walk

The way we walk through the world
Evidence of our hidden wings
Golden shadows of power
Made evident when we walk together

Song and dance
Art and poetry
Gifts of the Goddess
To bind us with hope

Dancing around the flowering tree
Rooted at the crossroad of eternity
Sisters of the moon gather
To manifest the birthing of harmony

Song and dance
Art and poetry
Gifts of the Goddess
To bind us with hope

When our loins open into pleasure
The sweet fragrant juices flowing
Lighting our eyes with desire
Our walk becomes a caress of time

Song and dance
Art and poetry
Gifts of the Goddess
To bind us with hope

Sisters of the moon gather
To praise each other's beauty
Empowering each other with laughter
Inspired by the way we walk

05JAN19

Six Lines #82

Smooth river stones nestle together
A small patch of river rocks
To connect with the subtle essence
Creek walking slowly and with care
Watching the glint of sunlight
Turning water into pure delight

04APR19

Psalm Of The Future

Oh, be you ready for it
When all those who bear the light
Stewards of the dawning age
Begin the task of shared minds
To manifest the purpose of the Universe
Opening the way for all of creation
To vibrate together in the great "I Know"

Oh, be you ready for it
When our water jeweled planet
Is birthed into Her true place among the stars
Her heart and soul reborn
To incandescent being
A key to the evolution of All That Is
For a future we can't yet comprehend

20MAR20

Embrace all the pain
Be with all of life's distress
Then welcome in joy

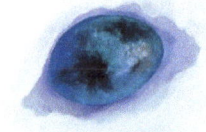

As The Ineffable Breathes

It's all here in each moment
Whether in pain or pleasure
The ineffable breathes
Animating even on this voracious
Star lighted orbing planet
We call our mother earth

All the conflicts of survival
Mitigated by the knowing
The All in all present
Even in our ignorance and fear
Beings of light and love
Breathing as the ineffable breathes

04MAR20

Stories At Midnight

Curled into the solace of midnight
After the wind has chilled the moonlight
I sit watching stories of dreamers
Listening to the kindness of affection
When the door in the wall is opened

Letting in the possible adversary
With an intention to create peace
Recognizing starlight even in conflict
I watch these examples of learning trust
Letting them shape me for sleep

I dream then of allies and joy
Untried avenues of cooperation
Begun when the fear of harm
Is replaced and hyper-vigilance abandoned
Rebelliousness recognized as self-protection

And midnight soothes the self-reproach
Smooths out the harshness of mistakes
Allowing the balm of forgiveness
With the possibilities of surrender
Stories written to show me another way

03FEB20

Beyond The Dark Wall

Soul decodes the unconscious
Beauty translates its form
The life-cycle of time
Arising and dissolving
In a rhythm of human breath

Breathe deeply into the now
Let its mysteries inform your life
For the brief brilliance it brings
Sweetened by the knowledge of death
Rising and dissolving beyond our reach

We cannot grasp and hold
What passes in an instant
The wheel of change ever revolving
Like prayer wheels in wind
Sending our entreaties to the ineffable

Take the moment to see what is
The mind unfolding into light and dark
To capture the fleeting senses
Sensate reality in Maya passing
Distinct and emergent as spirit

02JAN18

Pause

Fallow ground pauses
Soaking in air and energy
Subconscious beliefs slowly surface
While charismatics contend
For supremacy over the vulnerable

Again and again their voices bludgeon
A twenty-first century snake oil
Promising instant transformation
Wealth, health and the promise of love
To those who deem themselves unworthy

It's not news that a belief in brokenness
Results in looking outside oneself
Grasping at straws for answers
While the lessons of self-pacing and trust
Emerge from the chaos

And all ground needs fallow time
To regenerate and rest
Gathering in dreams and visions
To call into manifestation
That which grows within

15JUL18

Being Present

So often listening moves me
Off in the distance ravens cry
A grinding moan of streetcar
As it rounds a corner on its track
Punctuating distant hammering
While my clock patiently counts
Its ticking measuring time
And the subtle undercurrent
Urban drone to accompany sunlight
A plane roaring overhead
To the sound of dogs barking
My ears attuned to everyday miracles

24FEB20

:e of the Divine
ing shimmering alive
es beneath the moon

MAR20

Day Dream

When the day is slow
Sleep still tugging at your eyelids
Even though the sun is shining
Have a moment to reflect
In the still center of your reverie
Where future lovers congregate
And let yourself imagine

30JAN20

It's Already On Its Way

What would you want to greet
What would you like to see
Coming around that corner

Who would you choose to be
When the future unfolds for you
Bringing a chance for grace

How would you give more
Sharing your gifts and love
When what's coming arrives

07FEB20

Let It

Let it reach into your most protected corner
The one where your lost joy hides
Where your vulnerable side shivers
Behind the last wall of pain

Let it restore your trusting open heart
Soothing the wound with its touch
So that you can finally know in your bones
That Divine love and protection are for you

Let yourself embrace it
Let it sink into your soul
Let it guide you forward
Let it cherish you

26JAN20

A Practice Of Generosity

If you have no answers
Feel the breath of the Divine

Surrounding every small thing
Let grace mirror your face

Appreciating every blessing
That you awoke in the dawn

Clock ticking beside you
And there is food in the kitchen

Water and light and flowers
Even when you fear the unknown

Be willing to not know
Trusting what comes next

04OCT19

Three Sisters

They weave the fabric of time
What was, what is, what shall be
While I delve deeper into knowing

Gifted from the realms of departed souls
By beauty, generosity and devotion
I plumb the depths for tools

Awareness, allowing and acceptance
How to mine pain for treasure
As I sift and sort for alchemy

The past with its long shadow lessons
Reaches into the ever unfolding present
To sculpt and shape the possible future

Those three sisters of the Wyrd
Urda, Vedandi and Skuld weaving
And I keep shifting the lens for sight

02JAN19

Silver Snake Medicine

My mind rests in the winding
Sun shining on silvery waters
Rivers snaking through landscapes
Sharing their medicine with all
Sweet fluid for life and love

I daydream of silver snakes
Pillars of small painted shrines
Readying for inclusion of words
Found objects and fragments
Once buried after firestorms

Unearthed in transmuted forms
To give new meaning
From the ashes to the sacred
Devastation transformed
Rivers flowing through them all

13JUL18

Another Invocation of the Unknown

Moving past disappointment
Trust in synchronised timing
Open the doors of the unseen
Inviting in what you do not know

Let your inner voice sing of wisdom
Leading you into your own mystery
To find the unexpressed offerings
That trust lays open for your heart

Remember that you have not known
And disaster did not unfold
But Divine showered you with blessings
While your life moved forward

In these times of dire portent
When the world seems on fire
With corruption and cruelty
Seek inspiration in forgiveness

Let your knowing dance openly
With all you do not yet know
Finding what you can share
As you invoke the great Unknown

08OCT19

Deborah K. Tash
White Wolf Woman
In Her Image Studio
inherimage@artlover.com
www.inherimagestudio.com

Photography:
Donnie Felton/Almac Camera
M. Joseph Schaller, PhD
Deborah K. Tash

Deborah Karen Tash, White Wolf Woman, a Shamanic Artist, award winning poet and healer, is currently Artist In Residence for herchurch and curator of ARISE GALLERY in San Francisco, California.

Creating as a spiritual practice and means of self-expression has been the foundation of her work both as a visual artist and poet. She combines both whimsy and Shamanic influence on the path of beauty in her art.

Working in series she allows idea, inspiration and dreams to guide her in the choices she makes determining the kinds of medium and techniques to employ for each piece.

She works with painting, mixed media, sculpture, mask, drawing, fiber, collage, photography and clay often weaving them together in a single multimedia expression as well as writing poetry.

Deborah continues to explore how to use symbol and image in order to uncover the shape and influence of transformation on her interior life and that of the viewer, as well.

www.ingramcontent.com/pod-product-compliance
Lightning Source LLC
Chambersburg PA
CBHW040728150426
42811CB00063B/1538